All I want to do is stay in my knitwear, sit in front of the fireplace, pet my cat & reflect all day long

My Notes

My Notes

All I want to do is stay in my knitwear, sit in front of the fireplace, pet my cat & reflect all day long

My Notes

All I want to do is stay in my knitwear, sit in front of the fireplace, pet my cat & reflect all day long

My Notes

All I want to do is stay in my knitwear, sit in front of the fireplace, pet my cat & reflect all day long

My Notes

All I want to do is stay in my knitwear, sit in front of the fireplace, pet my cat & reflect all day long

My Notes

My Notes

All I want to do is stay in my knitwear, sit in front of the fireplace, pet my cat & reflect all day long

My Notes

All I want to do is stay in my knitwear, sit in front of the fireplace, pet my cat & reflect all day long

My Notes

All I want to do is stay in my knitwear, sit in front of the fireplace, pet my cat & reflect all day long

My Notes

All I want to do is stay in my knitwear, sit in front of the fireplace, pet my cat & reflect all day long

My Notes

My Notes

All I want to do is stay in my knitwear, sit in front of the fireplace, pet my cat & reflect all day long

My Notes

My Notes

All I want to do is stay in my knitwear, sit in front of the fireplace, pet my cat & reflect all day long

My Notes

All I want to do is stay in my knitwear, sit in front of the fireplace, pet my cat & reflect all day long

My Notes

All I want to do is stay in my knitwear, sit in front of the fireplace, pet my cat & reflect all day long

My Notes

All I want to do is stay in my knitwear, sit in front of the fireplace, pet my cat & reflect all day long

My Notes

My Notes

All I want to do is stay in my knitwear, sit in front of the fireplace, pet my cat & reflect all day long

My Notes

My Notes

All I want to do is stay in my knitwear, sit in front of the fireplace, pet my cat & reflect all day long

My Notes

My Notes

All I want to do is
stay in my knitwear,
sit in front of the
fireplace, pet my cat
& reflect all day long

My Notes

All I want to do is
stay in my knitwear,
sit in front of the
fireplace, pet my cat
& reflect all day long

My Notes

All I want to do is stay in my knitwear, sit in front of the fireplace, pet my cat & reflect all day long

My Notes

All I want to do is stay in my knitwear, sit in front of the fireplace, pet my cat & reflect all day long

My Notes

My Notes

All I want to do is
stay in my knitwear,
sit in front of the
fireplace, pet my cat
& reflect all day long

My Notes

My Notes

All I want to do is stay in my knitwear, sit in front of the fireplace, pet my cat & reflect all day long

My Notes

My Notes

All I want to do is stay in my knitwear, sit in front of the fireplace, pet my cat & reflect all day long

My Notes

All I want to do is
stay in my knitwear,
sit in front of the
fireplace, pet my cat
& reflect all day long

My Notes

All I want to do is
stay in my knitwear,
sit in front of the
fireplace, pet my cat
& reflect all day long

My Notes

My Notes

All I want to do is stay in my knitwear, sit in front of the fireplace, pet my cat & reflect all day long

My Notes

All I want to do is
stay in my knitwear,
sit in front of the
fireplace, pet my cat
& reflect all day long

My Notes

My Notes

All I want to do is stay in my knitwear, sit in front of the fireplace, pet my cat & reflect all day long

My Notes

My Notes

All I want to do is stay in my knitwear, sit in front of the fireplace, pet my cat & reflect all day long

My Notes

All I want to do is stay in my knitwear, sit in front of the fireplace, pet my cat & reflect all day long

My Notes

All I want to do is
stay in my knitwear,
sit in front of the
fireplace, pet my cat
& reflect all day long

My Notes

All I want to do is stay in my knitwear, sit in front of the fireplace, pet my cat & reflect all day long

My Notes

All I want to do is stay in my knitwear, sit in front of the fireplace, pet my cat & reflect all day long

My Notes

My Notes

All I want to do is stay in my knitwear, sit in front of the fireplace, pet my cat & reflect all day long

My Notes

My Notes

All I want to do is stay in my knitwear, sit in front of the fireplace, pet my cat & reflect all day long

My Notes

All I want to do is stay in my knitwear, sit in front of the fireplace, pet my cat & reflect all day long

My Notes

All I want to do is stay in my knitwear, sit in front of the fireplace, pet my cat & reflect all day long

My Notes

All I want to do is
stay in my knitwear,
sit in front of the
fireplace, pet my cat
& reflect all day long

My Notes

All I want to do is stay in my knitwear, sit in front of the fireplace, pet my cat & reflect all day long

My Notes

All I want to do is stay in my knitwear, sit in front of the fireplace, pet my cat & reflect all day long

My Notes

All I want to do is
stay in my knitwear,
sit in front of the
fireplace, pet my cat
& reflect all day long

My Notes

All I want to do is stay in my knitwear, sit in front of the fireplace, pet my cat & reflect all day long

My Notes

All I want to do is stay in my knitwear, sit in front of the fireplace, pet my cat & reflect all day long

My Notes

All I want to do is
stay in my knitwear,
sit in front of the
fireplace, pet my cat
& reflect all day long

My Notes

All I want to do is stay in my knitwear, sit in front of the fireplace, pet my cat & reflect all day long

My Notes

All I want to do is
stay in my knitwear,
sit in front of the
fireplace, pet my cat
& reflect all day long

My Notes

All I want to do is stay in my knitwear, sit in front of the fireplace, pet my cat & reflect all day long

My Notes

My Notes

All I want to do is
stay in my knitwear,
sit in front of the
fireplace, pet my cat
& reflect all day long

My Notes

All I want to do is stay in my knitwear, sit in front of the fireplace, pet my cat & reflect all day long

My Notes

All I want to do is
stay in my knitwear,
sit in front of the
fireplace, pet my cat
& reflect all day long

My Notes

All I want to do is stay in my knitwear, sit in front of the fireplace, pet my cat & reflect all day long

My Notes

All I want to do is stay in my knitwear, sit in front of the fireplace, pet my cat & reflect all day long

My Notes

My Notes

All I want to do is stay in my knitwear, sit in front of the fireplace, pet my cat & reflect all day long

My Notes

My Notes

All I want to do is stay in my knitwear, sit in front of the fireplace, pet my cat & reflect all day long

My Notes

All I want to do is stay in my knitwear, sit in front of the fireplace, pet my cat & reflect all day long

My Notes

All I want to do is stay in my knitwear, sit in front of the fireplace, pet my cat & reflect all day long

My Notes

All I want to do is stay in my knitwear, sit in front of the fireplace, pet my cat & reflect all day long

My Notes

My Notes

All I want to do is stay in my knitwear, sit in front of the fireplace, pet my cat & reflect all day long

My Notes

My Notes

All I want to do is
stay in my knitwear,
sit in front of the
fireplace, pet my cat
& reflect all day long

My Notes

My Notes

All I want to do is stay in my knitwear, sit in front of the fireplace, pet my cat & reflect all day long

My Notes

www.ingramcontent.com/pod-product-compliance
Lightning Source LLC
LaVergne TN
LVHW060333080526
838202LV00053B/4464